Shower of Blessings

Shower of Blessings

by Jamgön Mipham

with commentary by Lama Yeshe Gyamtso

KTD Publications
Woodstock New York

Published by:
KTD Publications
335 Meads Mountain Road
Woodstock, NY 12498, USA

www.KTDPublications.org

ISBN 978-1-934608-51-7
LCCN 2014937980

This book is printed on acid-free paper

Contents

Preface

Several years ago students requested that Khenpo Karthar Rinpoche, the abbot of Karma Triyana Dharmachakra Monastery in Woodstock, New York, provide them with a feast practice suitable for them to use on the tenth day of each lunar month, a day on which both feast practices and liturgies focused on Guru Padmasambhava are often performed. In response, he gave them Shower of Blessings.

Since then this practice has been performed as a tenth day observance monthly at KTD and at some of its affiliate centers. Since I had received detailed instruction on Shower of Blessings while serving as an interpreter for Khenpo Ugyen Trinley, a learned disciple of Khenpo Jigmey Phuntsok, I was assigned to teach it in September of 2007.

Since then several people have requested that the seminar be published as a book so that it might be readily available to the growing number of communities which perform this practice. This book is the result.

I would like to thank Khenchen Thrangu Rinpoche for transmitting Shower of Blessings, Khenpo Ugyen Trinley for explaining it,

Khenpo Karthar Rinpoche for encouraging students to practice it, Maureen McNicholas for editing this book, and Peter van Deurzen for both overseeing this publication and providing the beautiful painting on the front cover.

I hope that this book is helpful, especially to those who requested that it be published.

LYG

This book is dedicated to Khenchen Thrangu Rinpoche

Shower of Blessings
The Teaching

Introduction

Shower of Blessings is a guruyoga practice connected with Guru Rinpoche, Guru Padmasambhava, also called Padmakara. The practice was composed by Khenchen Mipham (1846-1912), a great master of the Nyingma tradition who also had great influence on the Karma Kagyu tradition. He spent several years of his life at Thrangu Monastery in East Tibet; consequently the scholarly tradition of the Karma Kagyu, especially through Khenchen Thrangu Rinpoche and other masters including Khenpo Karthar Rinpoche, is intimately connected with Mipham.

For many years Khenpo Karthar Rinpoche has been encouraging students to practice this guruyoga. In 1979 he presented a copy of this text to our center in Montreal. More recently, several of Rinpoche's disciples asked him for a liturgy that they could use as a feast practice on the tenth day, simple enough that everyone could practice it; his response was to recommend this guruyoga.

I received the transmission for the *Shower of Blessings* from Khenchen Thrangu Rinpoche. I received detailed instructions on it — the instructions which I will attempt to convey to you — from an eastern Tibetan lama called Khenpo Ogyen Trinley, a Nyingma khenpo who was trained by Khenpo Jigme Puntsok, a great master who founded a huge dharma encampment in eastern Tibet.

I would like to introduce the significance of this practice to you gradually before we go into detail. The first thing we need to look at is the importance of guruyoga in general. Many of the practices we do are guruyoga. It is the last of the four preliminaries. In addition to that, in the Karma Kagyu tradition we also practice guruyogas of Marpa, Milarepa, Gampopa, and Karma Pakshi, the Second Karmapa. We also practice many different forms of Guru Rinpoche guruyoga.

What is guruyoga? *Guru* means "spiritual teacher." *Yoga* can be used to mean many kinds of practice, but has the connotation of "union." In essence guruyoga is any practice you do in order to mix your mind with the mind of your guru. It can be focused on your guru as he or she appears to you, but is often focused on your guru inseparable from a lineage figure such as Vajradhara, Guru Rinpoche, Marpa, Milarepa, or Gampopa.

What does mixing your mind and the mind of your guru mean? Are you really taking two different things and mixing them? No. Mixing your mind and the mind of your guru is recognizing the nature of your mind through devotion to your guru. Since the nature of your guru's mind is the same as the nature of your mind, when you recognize that nature you also recognize their unity of nature.

You may find this idea surprising. Are we not encouraged to think of the great difference between ourselves and our guru? The guru is an awakened being, the embodiment of compassion and wisdom; we are samsaric beings who depend upon the guru. We are also taught that devotion is marked by humility, and never by the arrogance of thinking that one is the guru's equal. That is very true, but the purpose of humility in devotion is to become open to the guru's wisdom. Although in the practice of guruyoga we acknowledge the apparent separation between the guru and the disciple, one of the practice's purposes is to break through that very sense of separation. This is possible because our minds are already identical in nature to the mind of our guru.

To understand this we must learn to distinguish between our deluded minds and their nature. Our delusion is not identical to our guru's mind; our guru is our guru because he or she is free from delusion. The nature of our minds, however, is no different than the nature of our guru's mind. He or she has recognized that nature and is free from delusion; we have not recognized that nature and remain deluded. We practice guruyoga in order to become like our guru: free from delusion.

As deluded as our minds are, in nature they are nothing other than emptiness that knows. Our minds are empty, just like everything else. What makes a mind different from any other empty thing is that although it is empty, it knows; it experiences. That is what our minds really are, and that is what our guru's mind is. Therefore the main difference between us and our guru is that our guru sees his or her own mind exactly as it is and we, as yet, do not. The mind that each of us has, that we don't recognize; and the mind that the guru has, that he or she does recognize, are identical. Because guruyoga helps us recognize our mind's nature through devotion, the importance of guruyoga practice can never be overestimated. In the tantras it is said that it is better to meditate on the single form of one's guru than to meditate on a million deities; it is better to mix one's mind with the guru's for even a moment than to meditate on the completion stage for a million kalpas. Because the easiest way, some would say the only way, to recognize the nature of one's mind is through devotion, it is said that the best devotion leads to the best meditation; mediocre devotion leads to mediocre meditation; and poor devotion leads to poor meditation. That is one of the main reasons we practice guruyoga.

Among guruyogas, why practice a guruyoga focused on the historical figure of Guru Rinpoche, Guru Padmasambhava? There are two reasons. The first reason is that Guru Rinpoche is an emanation of the Buddha who appeared in order to teach the vajrayana or tantra; this is why we often call Guru Rinpoche the Second Buddha.

The second reason for our veneration of Guru Rinpoche is that his particular activity is the activity which is needed when dharma moves from one culture to another. We therefore regard many of the great masters of many Buddhist traditions as emanations of Guru Rinpoche, Padmasambhava.

It takes a certain type of teacher to actually bridge the tremendous gap between cultures. One thing that such a teacher must be able to do is subdue the arrogance of the receiving culture. All cultures regard anything foreign, including Buddhism initially, with suspicion. Guru Rinpoche overcame the resistance among Tibetan people and spirits to the Buddhist message of universal compassion; we therefore seek his blessing so that we may overcome our resistance to it. We can only overcome our pride, cultural and personal, through devotion.

The quality which enables a teacher to bring dharma into a receiving culture is warm compassion. We frequently speak of Guru Rinpoche's miraculous powers, but it is important to remember that beings like Guru Rinpoche and the Gyalwang Karmapa are powerful because they are perfectly compassionate; they are truly perfect embodiments of compassion. By venerating Guru Rinpoche we invoke that warmth in order to melt the ice of our rigid selfhood, the identity that we cling to.

The focus of this practice is a prayer called the Seven-Line Supplication or the Seven-Line Prayer. It is recited at the beginning of the practice, together with the supplication to the Tibetan master Yeshe Tsogyal, and is also accumulated as the central part of the practice. We will begin by looking at these two prayers. Then we will go through the meaning and visualizations of the practice.

The Seven-Line Supplication

The first of these two supplications, the Seven-Line Supplication, is generally considered to be the most important of all the prayers to Guru Rinpoche. We should probably begin by looking at its history.

Guru Rinpoche first appeared on a lotus flower in a lake, probably in what is now Pakistan, which was then called Uddiyana. This prayer was sung to him then by various dakinis, enlightened female beings, as an invitation to appear in the world. It later reappeared at Nalanda Monastery. Nalanda was one of the main monastic and scholarly institutions of Indian Buddhism. Naropa taught there, as did many other great masters. The ruins of Nalanda are still there; I went there on pilgrimage in 1986.

Debates between Buddhists and non-Buddhists were apparently common at Nalanda. There was some risk involved, in that these debates seem to have been public. If Buddhists began to regularly lose every debate they entered, people might begin to wonder about the authenticity of the Buddhadharma.

The story of the Seven-Line Supplication at Nalanda is this: At one time the five hundred mahapanditas of Nalanda had reached the point where their Hindu challengers were winning every debate. One night all of these worried panditas had the same dream. A dakini appeared to them and said, "None of you are able to defeat these challengers in debate; only my brother is!"

In their dream each of the panditas asked the dakini, "How can we invite your brother here?"

She said to each of them, "You must all go up onto the roof of the central temple and call to him with these words." Then she taught them the Seven-Line Supplication.

The next morning they all discovered that they had had the same dream, so they went up onto the roof of the central temple, set out elaborate offerings, and recited the Seven-Line Supplication. Guru Rinpoche appeared in their midst and single-handedly defeated all the challengers in debate.

The Seven-Line Supplication is also a treasure or terma discovered by the early treasure revealer Guru Chökyi Wangchuk; it is found in his *Guru Guhyasamaja*. In that cycle it is written that if you recite this prayer with sincerity Guru Rinpoche has no choice but to actually come to you.

The Seven-Line Supplication is extraordinary. It is an affirmation of Guru Rinpoche's greatness, a prayer for his blessing, and an invitation to him to come to you. It can be recited by itself, at the beginning of another practice, or in the context of this guruyoga.

The prayer begins with the syllable HUM, which represents the five wisdoms and therefore the mind of all buddhas. We recite this syllable at the beginning of the prayer to invoke Guru Rinpoche's enlightened mind. The first line is:

Orgyen yül gyi nup jang tsam,
At the northwest border of the land of Uddiyana.

Uddiyana is an old name for what is now probably part of

Pakistan. A long time ago it served as the home of the vajrayana teachings. Many of the original tantras were brought to Central India from Uddiyana. It was also where Guru Rinpoche made his initial appearance. Although the text seems to be saying in the northwest border of Uddiyana, it means "Uddiyana, in the northwest of the Indian subcontinent." So the first line tells us where Guru Rinpoche first appeared. The second line is:

> Padma ge sar dong po la,
> On the center of a lotus stalk.

The stalk is mentioned to show that it is a living lotus flower and that Guru Rinpoche was found on top of the center of it. Gesar means the "center of a flower." The third line is:

> Ya tsen chok gi ngö drup nye,
> You achieved amazing supreme siddhi.

Guru Rinpoche achieved the amazing supreme siddhi of perfect awakening. The placement of this third line after the second indicates that he achieved it at the time of his first appearance, or had already achieved it by then. The fourth line is:

> Padma jung ne zhe su drak,
> You are called Padmakara.

Padmakara means Lotus Origin. Guru Rinpoche bears that name because he first appeared on a lotus. The fifth line is:

> Khor du khandro mang pö kor,
> You are surrounded by many dakinis.

The sixth line is:

> Kye kyi je su dak drup kyi,
> I follow your example in practice and accomplishment.

The seventh line is:

> Jin gyi lap chir she su söl,
> I pray that you come here to grant your blessing.

We need to look closely at the connection between the sixth and seventh lines. The sixth line is very important because it affirms the basis of our petition or supplication. In the seventh line we ask Guru Rinpoche to come to us and bless us. The importance of the sixth line is that it affirms the reason for our confidence that Guru Rinpoche will do so. Awakened beings bless everyone, but to receive their blessing we must be seeking to emulate them. Because we are emulating Guru Rinpoche by practicing, he can and therefore will bless us.

This prayer is a bit like a letter. The first five lines remind us of Guru Rinpoche's magnificence, and are like the address and salutation at the top of a letter. The sixth line is our explanation, the reason for our request. It is like writing, "I am trying to do what you have done, but I need your help." The seventh line is our actual request: "I pray that you come here to grant your blessing." We conclude the prayer with Guru Rinpoche's name mantra GURU PADMA SIDDHI HUM. *Siddhi* means "attainment," so this mantra is another way to ask for his blessing so that we may gain the attainment that he embodies.

The sign of receiving the blessing of Guru Rinpoche or of any awakened being is that we change for the better. If we do not improve, we are not receiving the blessing of an awakened being. This prayer also has several further layers of meaning. To learn about them, I suggest you read Mipham Rinpoche's *White Lotus*, which is a complete explanation of all levels of the prayer's meaning. The Padmakara Translation Committee has translated it and it has been published by Shambhala Publications.

The Supplication of Yeshe Tsogyal

The other prayer that is recited before the main practice is a prayer to Yeshe Tsogyal composed by the Fifteenth Gyalwang Karmapa Khakyap Dorje. Yeshe Tsogyal was a Tibetan noblewoman from one of the sixth main ruling clans of that land. She became Guru Rinpoche's foremost disciple. Among her many other qualities she had an eidetic memory and was therefore able to retain all of the teachings she heard or read. She is considered to have been an emanation of Sarasvati, the goddess of learning, and also of Vajrayogini. She achieved perfect awakening and was therefore one of the first generation of Tibetan Buddhists who achieved the supreme attainment. She was also Guru Rinpoche's spiritual consort while he was in Tibet. The first line of her supplication or prayer is:

Gyal kün kye yum chö ying kün zang mo,
Mother of all buddhas, dharmadhatu, Samantabhadri.

Every buddha becomes a buddha by perfectly realizing the nature of all things, dharmata. Because dharmata is the nature of all things without exception, it is also called the dharmadhatu, the "expanse of all things." The dharmadhatu is not just emptiness; it is inseparable from the wisdom that realizes it. Why? The wisdom that realizes absolute truth is a self-aware wisdom, not a dualistic cognition. Therefore the object of that wisdom is the nature of that wisdom itself. We therefore call the dharmadhatu the Mother of All Buddhas, since its realisation is the birth of buddhahood. Because the realizing wisdom, the dharmakaya, is inseparable from the realized dharmadhatu, we also call the dharmadhatu Samantabhadri, which is a feminine name for the dharmakaya. When someone achieves buddhahood they become the wisdom-dharmakaya; since Yeshe Tsogyal achieved the wisdom-dharmakaya, she is Samantabhadri, inseparable from the dharmadhatu. The second line is:

> Bö bang kyop pay ma chik drin mo che,
> Only kind mother and protector of Tibetans.

"Only kind mother" means that she is like the mother of all of her followers, Tibetans and others. She protects us both from lower rebirth and from problems in this life. The third line is:

> Ngö drup chok tsöl de chen khandroi tso,
> Bestower of supreme siddhi, foremost dakini of mahasukha.

Yeshe Tsogyal embodies not only the wisdom of the dharmadhatu but the affect of that wisdom, which is mahasukha, great bliss. Yeshe Tsogyal bestows supreme siddhi by blessing those who are devoted to her. The fourth line is:

> Ye she tso gyal zhap la söl wa deb,
> I supplicate at the feet of Yeshe Tsogyal.

This means that you are praying to her with great respect.

The fifth line specifies what you are praying for. It says:

> Chi nang sang way bar che zhi wa dang,
> Pacify outer, inner, and secret obstacles.

Outer obstacles are problems in the external world such as warfare and environmental disasters. Inner obstacles are physical problems and sickness. Secret obstacles are our kleshas and mental problems. The sixth line is:

> La may ku tse ten par jin gyi lop,
> Grant your blessing so that the gurus' lives may be stable.

We are asking her to ensure that our gurus live long and that their health is good. The seventh line is:

> Ne muk tsön kel zhi bar jin gyi lop,
> Bless us that this age of sickness, famine, and war be pacified.

This is easy to understand. The eighth line is:

> Je phur bö tong zhi war jin gyi lop,
> Bless us that curses, kila-magic, and incitements be pacified.

This is asking her to protect us from others' curses. The ninth line is:

> Tse pel she rap gye par jin gyi lop
> Bless us that life, wealth, and wisdom increase.

"Life" means vitality as well as the length of life. "Wealth" means affluence and resources. "Wisdom" means both intelligence and knowledge. The tenth and last line is:

> Sam pa lhun gyi drup par jin gyi lop,
> Bless us so that our wishes may be spontaneously fulfilled.

We conclude the prayer by asking her to cause all of our wishes to be fulfilled without effort or struggle.

This prayer is recited once at the beginning of the session; then we begin the main guruyoga.

The Guruyoga

The main practice begins with the word AH. AH is considered to be the most fundamental unit of language; it is regarded as the fundamental sound. Although AH is a sound, it represents the uncreated or unborn. Saying AH at the beginning indicates that we are going to be meditating on the ultimate nature of all things in the form of our guru inseparable from Guru Rinpoche. The first line is:

Rang lü ta mel ne pay dün kha ru,
In the sky before my ordinary form.

In this practice we do not visualize ourselves as a deity. The next line is:

Orgyen dri me dha na ko shay tso,
Is the stainless Lake Dhanakosha of Uddiyana.

Imagine that the entire realm of Uddiyana appears in the sky in front of you. In its center is the vast, peaceful, and beautiful Lake Dhanakosha.

I should mention that although Uddiyana used to be a name for what is now part of Pakistan, you are not imagining that country. You are imagining the pure realm of Uddiyana, the celestial realm of Uddiyana, the realm of the vidyadharas and dakinis. The next line is:

> Ting zap yen lak gye den chü gang way,
> It is deep and filled with water of eight attributes.

The eight attributes of the water in Lake Dhanakosha are sweetness, coolness, softness, lightness, transparency, purity, being pleasant to swallow, and being beneficial to the stomach. The next line is:

> Ü su rin chen pe dong dab gye teng,
> In its midst is a precious lotus in bloom.

The stalk of this lotus flower is very large, like the trunk of a tree. Its petals are innumerable and of all colors. The lotus is made entirely of jewels; it is a living flower yet made of jewels. All its blue petals are made of sapphire, and yet flexible and soft. All its red petals are made of ruby, all the white ones of quartz crystal or diamond, the green ones of emerald, and the yellow ones of topaz.

The center of the flower is covered by two cushions that are perfect circles. The first is the sun. It is not a sphere, but a disk of brilliant yellow or orange light. On top of it is the moon, which is also not a sphere and not full of holes and grey spots and so on; it is a perfect disk of cooling white light. The next line is:

> Kyap ne kün dü orgyen dorje chang,
> Atop is Uddiyana Vajradhara who embodies all refuges.

Seated in vajra posture on the lotus, sun, and moon is Guru Rinpoche in the form of Uddiyana Vajradhara. There are many forms of Guru Rinpoche; this is one of them. I have seen thangkas depicting this form, exactly as it is described in this liturgy, and I will describe him accordingly.

Guru Rinpoche embodies all sources of refuge. His mind is the Buddha, the dharmakaya, the true Buddha. His speech is the dharma. His body is the sangha. All yidams are his qualities. All protectors are his activity. The next line is:

Tsen pay pal bar tso gyal yum dang tril,
With splendid marks and signs he embraces the
    mother Tsogyal.

Guru Rinpoche is in the sambhogakaya form of Uddiyana Vajradhara, the form he took when he received the eighteen maha-yoga tantras from the dharmakaya Buddha Samantabhadra. He is deep blue, royal blue, and luminous and possesses the thirty-two marks and eighty signs of a Buddha. He wears the sambhogakaya ornaments. Half of his long hair flows down over his shoulders to represent that he does not abandon sentient beings by remaining in solitary nirvana. Half of it is bound up in a top knot, which represents that in spite of not abandoning sentient beings he is himself completely free of samsara. As a peaceful sambhogakaya he wears thirteen adornments: eight articles of jewelry, and five articles of clothing. These indicate that he has transcended existence and tranquility, samsara and nirvana.

His first article of jewelry is his crown or tiara. This includes a wish-fulfilling jewel, like a large sapphire, at the peak of his top-knot. Mounted on the tiara, on his forehead, are five drop-shaped diadems. They are made of gold. Within each of them is a jewel of one of the five colors. They represent the five wisdoms.

His second ornament is earrings, also made of gold and jewels. His third, fourth, and fifth ornaments are necklaces: a short one close to his throat, a longer one that hangs down to his solar plexus, and an even longer one that hangs to his waist. These are also made of gold and jewels. Finally, he has bracelets on his upper arms, at his wrists, and at his ankles; these are the sixth, seventh, and eighth ornaments and are also made of gold and jewels.

Uddiyana Vajradhara is wearing five garments. The first is the silk ribbon that binds his topknot. The second is the red silk diadem or ribbon that binds his tiara together at the back of his head; it is tied in a bow. The third is a longer and wider silk ribbon, usually shown as blue or green. It flows over his shoulders like an ornamental scarf. The fourth is his blouse or shirt. It covers his upper body from his throat to his solar plexus, has wide short sleeves, and is made of white silk decorated with designs sewn in gold thread. The fifth is his skirt, which is of red silk and also decorated with designs sewn in gold thread. These are called the thirteen adornments of the peaceful sambhogakaya.

Uddiyana Vajradhara is embracing Yeshe Tsogyal. She is brilliant white tinged with red, seated in Guru Rinpoche's lap with her legs around his waist. She holds a hooked knife in her right hand, which is wrapped around Guru Rinpoche's neck. Her left hand holds a skull cup filled with amrita, which is a transparent liquid that radiates five colors of light and bestows immortality and wisdom. She is wearing the same type of jewelry and clothing as Uddiyana Vajradhara, although some of her jewelry is made from bone, which represents the wisdom of bliss-emptiness. The next line is:

Chak ye dorje yön pay tö bum nam,
His right hand holds a vajra, his left a skull and vase.

In his right hand Uddiyana Vajradhara holds a five-pronged golden vajra in front of his heart with his palm facing outward in the gesture of protection. In his left hand he holds a skull cup in the gesture of meditation. Inside the skull cup is a longevity vase. In other practices Uddiyana Vajradhara holds a vajra and bell, but in this guruyoga he holds a vajra, skull, and vase like other forms of Guru Rinpoche. The vajra and skull represent his achievement of perfect compassion and wisdom; the vase represents his achievement of immortality. The next line is:

Dar dang rin chen rü pay gyen gyi dze,
They are adorned by silk, jewels, and bone.

This was explained earlier. The next line is:

Ö ngay long ne de chen zi jin bar,
In an expanse of the five lights, they blaze with great bliss.

Their bodies emit brilliant light of five colors: white, red, blue, yellow, and green. This light represents their five wisdoms. They blaze with great bliss because they have eradicated ignorance, the cause of suffering. To indicate that awakening is blissful, they are in union. The next line is:

Khor du tsa sum gyamtso trin tar tib,
The oceans of the three roots surround them like clouds.

Oceans and clouds here have the significance of "many." They are surrounded by many gurus, many yidams, and many dakinis and dharmapalas. Above Guru Rinpoche are all the lineage gurus; Guru Rinpoche himself is identified with your root guru. Surrounding Guru Rinpoche and Yeshe Tsogyal are all the yidams, the peaceful and wrathful deities. Beneath Guru Rinpoche and

Yeshe Tsogyal are all the dharma protectors and dakinis. The next line is:

> Jin lap tuk je char beb dak la zik,
> Raining down blessing and compassion, he gazes at me.

Guru Rinpoche is gazing right at us with love and compassion.

The Seven Branches

Then we begin the seven branches of accumulation. The first of the seven branches, homage or prostration, is described in the next two lines:

Gyal kün ngo wo chi me ye she kur
Dung shuk drak pö de chak tak tu tsal,

To the immortal wisdom body of all victors
I will always prostrate with intense faith and yearning.

We devotedly prostrate to Guru Rinpoche and his entourage with countless imagined replicas of our own bodies, recognizing that he embodies the wisdom of all Buddhas. Prostration, the first of the seven branches, is a remedy for the affliction of pride. It therefore serves both to accumulate merit and to purify obscurations. This is true of the remaining six branches as well.

The second of the seven branches, offering, is described in the next two lines:

Lü dang long chö dü sum ge way tsok
Kün zang chö pay trin du mik ne bül,

I offer my body, possessions, and virtues of the three times,
Imagining them as Samantabhadra's offering clouds.

Since offering is a remedy for attachment, we offer those things to which we are most attached: our bodies; our possessions; and everything good we have ever done, are doing, or will ever do. In order to accumulate as much merit as possible, we multiply each thing we offer in our imaginations as many times as we can. The bodhisattva Samantabhadra miraculously multiplied every offering he presented to the point of infinity; we emulate him through imagination and aspiration. Offering, the second of the seven branches, is a remedy for the affliction of attachment.

The third branch is confession. It is described in the next line:

Tok me ne sak dik tung ma lü shak,
I confess all wrongdoing and downfalls performed throughout
   beginningless time.

We confess actions of two types: wrongdoing and downfalls. Wrongdoing includes all actions that are wrong even if we have not vowed not to do them. For example, killing is wrong even if we've never taken a vow not to kill. Downfalls are violations of any virtuous vow we have made in the presence of the three jewels. We do not remember all of our beginningless wrongdoing, so we make our confession all-inclusive. Confession, the third of the seven branches, is a remedy for anger, as well as for the karmic obscuration.

The fourth branch is rejoicing in others' goodness. This is described in the next two and one half lines.

Se che gyal wa kün gyi yön ten gyi
Kyap dak chik pu gön po'i nam tar la

Nying ne yi rang,
I rejoice from my heart in your deeds,
Only all-pervasive lord of the virtues of all victors
    and their children.

The "only all-pervasive lord" refers to Guru Rinpoche, who is the all-pervasive overlord in the sense that he embodies in his person all of the qualities of all victors and their children. By rejoicing in Guru Rinpoche's virtue, we are also rejoicing in all of the virtue performed by anyone, because he embodies all of it. Rejoicing, the fourth branch, is a remedy for the affliction of jealousy.

The fifth branch is described in the rest of the line we just began:

De pe söl deb shing,
I pray to you with faith.

Often this branch is a prayer that Buddhas, bodhisattvas, and gurus remain in the world, and that they not pass into parinirvana. In that case this branch is a remedy for the affliction of wrong views, and in particular the misapprehension of things as permanent. Since Guru Rinpoche has achieved immortality, in this case this branch is simply praying to him with great faith. Faith is the main remedy for the affliction of wrong views, and in particular the wrong view that the three jewels lack the attributes ascribed to them.

The sixth branch is the request that the wheel of dharma be turned. The next line is:

Zap gye chö kyi char chen beb par kül,
I request that you shower us with dharma both
    profound and vast.

The sixth branch, the request that the wheel of dharma be turned, is a remedy for the affliction of ignorance.

The final branch of the seven is the dedication of virtue, which is described in the next four lines:

Rang zhen ge way ngö po kün dom ne
Dro kham gyamtso ji si ne kyi bar
Gön po kyö kyi nam tar je nyek te
Kha kyap dro wa dren pay dön du ngo,

I dedicate all the virtue of myself and others to this:
For as long as the oceans of beings remain,
May I emulate your deeds, my lord,
And be a guide to all beings throughout space.

We dedicate all of our virtue and all of the virtue of others to our becoming a guide of beings like Guru Rinpoche, and continuing to guide beings until they have all achieved buddhahood. The seventh branch, dedication, is a remedy for the affliction of greed or selfishness.

The seven branches are seven ways to accumulate merit and also remedies for seven types of affliction: pride, attachment, anger, jealousy, wrong views, ignorance, and selfishness.

The Main Practice of Supplication

Having now accumulated merit and purified ourselves, we begin the main practice of supplication, which has two parts: a supplication of eight lines that is recited once, and the repetition of the Seven-Line Supplication for the bulk of the session. The first line of the initial supplication is:

Kyap ne kün dü kyen tsey ter chen po,
Embodiment of all refuges, great treasury of wisdom and love.

Guru Rinpoche embodies all sources of refuge and is therefore filled with both impartial love and perfect wisdom, like an inexhaustible treasury. The next line is:

Dü ngen nyik may kyap chok rin po che,
Invaluable protector of beings during bad and decadent times.

Guru Rinpoche is said to be especially powerful in bad times, when the length and quality of life diminish, when the environment is becoming polluted, when our kleshas are becoming coarser, and when our views are becoming more and more confused. At such times he is said to be an especially powerful protector of beings. The next line is:

> Nga do gü pe nar shing dung shuk kyi,
> With my mind tormented by fivefold degeneration.

We are desperate, tormented by the degeneration of ourselves, our lives, our environment, our kleshas, and our views. The next line is:

> Söl deb bü la tse we tuk kyi gong,
> Consider with love this child who prays to you.

The meaning of this is clear. The next line is:

> Gong pay long ne tuk jey tsal chung la,
> From the expanse of your wisdom, unleash the power of your
>   compassion.

This line reminds us that Guru Rinpoche's compassion is the natural display of his wisdom; they are not separate. The next line is:

> Mö den dak gi nying la jin gyi lop.
> I am devoted to you; bless my heart.

This line reminds us that it is our devotion that makes us receptive to blessing. The next line is:

> Tak dang tsen ma nyur du tön pa dang,
> Quickly display signs and indications.

We ask for signs of his blessing, so that our faith may increase. The last line of this section is:

> Chok dang tün mong ngö drup tsel du söl,
> I pray that you grant supreme and common siddhis.

Supreme siddhi is awakening; common siddhis include longevity, prosperity, health, charisma, and so on. We gain siddhi by receiving Guru Rinpoche's blessing and becoming more like him: more compassionate, wiser, and closer to awakening.

As for the repetitions, the principal one is the Seven-Line Supplication. Toward the end of the session we also recite the twelve-syllable VAJRA GURU mantra. While reciting them think that from the hearts of Guru Rinpoche and Yeshe Tsogyal and also from the juncture of their union rays or strings of bright, five-colored light shoot out and dissolve into your heart, granting you their blessing.

The text you have before you is actually three texts spliced together: the guruyoga, a feast liturgy written by Mipham for this guruyoga, and a short feast liturgy for repetition. For daily practice one would usually omit the feast, which is usually practiced on the tenth day of the lunar month. When omitting the feast, after the recitation of the accumulation of the Seven-Line Supplication and the VAJRA GURU mantra one simply concludes the practice with the empowerment, dissolution, and dedication. Since we are primarily concerned here with the tenth day celebration, we will turn now to the feast practice.

The Feast

This guruyoga is called *Rain of Blessings* or *Shower of Blessings*; its feast liturgy is called *The Glorious Excellent Vase*. A vase represents an inexhaustible source of good things, like a cornucopia. Similarly, feast practice is considered to be the best way to accumulate merit. As Yeshe Tsogyal wrote, "Among the means of gathering the accumulations, ganachakra is supreme." Feast practice not only accumulates merit; it restores one's purity of outlook and therefore repairs samaya.

The Sanskrit terms for feast practice are *ganachakra*, "gathering wheel," and *ganapuja*, "gathering offering." In either case, "gathering" refers to four gatherings. First is the gathering of deities to whom the feast is offered. Second is the gathering of yogins and yoginis who make the offerings. Third is the gathering of samaya substances as offerings, which means both food and drink. Fourth is the resultant gathering of the accumulations. Through offering food and drink to the deities one gathers the accumulations of both merit and wisdom. All four of these gatherings are the nonduality of upaya and prajna in nature. The deities are male and female, embodiments of compassion and wisdom. The practitioners are male yogins and female yoginis. The food and drink offered represent means and wisdom. The accumulations of merit and wisdom are also upaya and prajna respectively.

The feast begins with the consecration of the feast offerings. The first line is:

> HUM. A le chö ying dang nyam ka pa lar,
> HUM. From AH arises a kapala equal to the dharmadhatu.

From the syllable AH appears a skull-cup the size of the entire universe. It is in front of us, between us and Guru Rinpoche. Why a skull-cup? According to His Holiness the Dalai Lama, the channels and essences which produce the experience of bliss are toward the top of the brain, inside our skulls. The skull therefore represents bliss. It also represents emptiness because it is a sign of impermanence. Impermanence is evidence of emptiness. If things were inherently existent, they would not be subject to conditions and would therefore never change.

As a sign of bliss the kapala is white on the outside; as a sign of emptiness it is red on the inside. As a sign of the single nature of all things it is in one piece, undivided by sutures or cracks. It appears from a white AH syllable because that syllable represents the unborn nature of all things. Something that truly exists must have been truly born, must have truly come into existence. If nothing exists inherently, there can be no true birth or production. Therefore the skull-cup, arisen from AH, also represents the magical illusion of appearances. The next line is:

> OM le nang si dö yön tsok su shom,
> From OM arises all that appears and exists, set out as a
>   desirable feast.

Inside the kapala is a white OM radiating five colored light. It becomes the feast substances in the form of everything that is pleasing to the five senses. You can imagine this as an ocean of amrita from which everything desirable is emanated. The next line is:

HUM gi de chen ye she röl par gyur,
With HUM it is transformed into the play of the wisdom of
    great bliss.

Above the amrita appears a blue HUM syllable. HUM represents the five wisdoms of all buddhas. The HUM melts into light and dissolves into the amrita, making it inseparable from the wisdom of all Buddhas. The next line is:

HRI yi tsa sum tsok gye pa kang,
With HRI the deities of the three roots are filled with
    pleasure.

Above the amrita appears a HRI syllable, white or of five colors. It dissolves into the amrita, causing it to expand endlessly, to emanate countless other offerings and gods and goddesses holding countless offerings. All of these things fill the sky, satisfying all of the innumerable deities of the three roots.

We then recite the mantra OM AH HUM HRI three times in order to bless the feast offerings. This mantra represents the body, speech, mind, and wisdom of all Buddhas. It also represents the purification and consecration of the feast vessels as a kapala, of the feast offerings as amrita, of that amrita as wisdom, and of that wisdom amrita as a boundless display.

We then invite the field of accumulation. The invitation begins with the Seven-Line Supplication, used here as a feast invitation.

You will notice that a couple of lines are different in this case. Up to the sixth line, "I follow your example in accomplishment," the prayer is the same. The seventh line, however, is:

Dö yön tsok la chen dren na,
If I invite you to this desirable feast.

This is followed by an eighth line:

Jin gyi lop chir shek su söl,
I pray that you come here to grant your blessing.

The remaining lines in the invitation describe the descent of blessings. The next line is:

Ne chok di ru jin pop la,
Rain down blessings on this best of places.

We call the place where we are practicing the best of places because it is being consecrated as a glorious feast hall of dakas and dakinis. The next line is:

Tsok chö ye she dü tsir gyur,
Transform these feast offerings into wisdom amrita.

We have blessed the offerings with mantra and our imagination; now we ask Guru Rinpoche to bless them with his authentic wisdom. The next line is:

Drup chok dak la wang zhi kur,
Grant me, a supreme practitioner, the four empowerments.

Why do we call ourselves supreme practitioners? Because we are practitioners of guruyoga, the supreme practice. We are praising the dharma we practice, not ourselves. The four empowerments are: the vase empowerment of body, the secret empowerment of speech, the knowledge-wisdom empowerment of mind, and the word empowerment of awareness-display. The next line is:

Gek dang lok dren bar che söl,
Remove obstructors, corruptors, and impediments.

Obstructors are malevolent beings who attempt to impede our achievement of buddhahood. Corruptors are beings who mislead others spiritually. Impediments are obstacles of any kind to awakening. The next line is:

Chok dang tün mong ngö drup tsöl,
Grant supreme and common siddhi.

We ask Guru Rinpoche to bestow supreme and common attainments. That completes the invitation.

Next is the presentation of the feast offerings. In many feasts the offering is divided into three phases: the presentation of the select portion, the fulfillment offering, and the liberation offering. These are all included in this liturgy, although they are not presented here as separate offerings. The first line of the offering liturgy is:

Hum la ma je tsün padma tö treng tsel,
Hum Guru, Lord Padma Tötrengtsal.

Tötreng means "garland of skulls." Padma Tötreng is one of Guru Rinpoche's names. Tsel means "powerful." The second line is:

Rik dzin khandro tsok dang che pa yi,
With your assembly of vidyadharas and dakinis.

Vidyadharas are tantric gurus. The next line is:

35

Tsa sum kün dü gyal way kyil khor la,
To the mandala of victors that embodies all the three roots.

Guru Rinpoche and his entourage embody and include all
Buddhas or victors and all of the three roots. The next line is:

Mö gü dung shuk drag pö söl wa deb,
I pray with intense devotion and yearning.

This is easy to understand. The next three lines are:

Dak zhen go sum ge tsok long chö che
Nang si dö yön gye gu ma tsang me
Kün zang de chen tsok kyi kor lor bül

I offer you my own and others' three gates, virtues, and
    possessions;
All appearance and existence; and everything desirable
    and pleasing,
As a ganachakra of Samantabhadra's great bliss.

Our feast offering includes everything that exists. We can offer
everything that exists to Guru Rinpoche because no one loses anything through our doing so. For example, if I offer another person's virtues to a Buddha or bodhisattva, that other person does
not lose any of their virtue; in addition to their virtue they now
have a karmic connection with that Buddha or bodhisattva.

By offering everything, we accumulate great merit. But our
offering of everything is special in another way: we offer everything as "a ganachakra of Samantabhadra's great bliss."
Samantabhadra refers here to the dharmakaya. A Buddha experiences everything as utterly pure, and is free from suffering.
So when we offer everything that exists in this way, we are offering everything as experienced by a Buddha. This means that our

offering is not only unlimited, in that it is all-inclusive; it is also utterly pure. The next line is:

Tuk tsey gye zhe tuk dam kang gyur chik,
Kindly accept it. May my commitments to you be fulfilled.

Through these offerings, may my samaya with you be restored. The second part of this line also has the connotation of "May you be satisfied." Guru Rinpoche and other Buddhas are most satisfied when we fulfill our samaya and are able to approach awakening. They accept our offerings for our sake, not theirs. The following lines are:

Söl wa dep so gu ru rin po che,
Chin gyi lop shik rig dzin khandro tsok,
Mö den bu la chok tün ngö drup tsöl,
Dam tsik nyam chak tam che jang du söl,

Guru Rinpoche, I pray to you;
Bless me, vidyadharas and dakinis;
Grant your devoted child supreme and common siddhi;
I pray that you purify all violations of samaya.

These lines expand upon the meaning of the previous line, and constitute the equivalent in this liturgy of the second feast offering, the fulfillment offering. The next line is:

Chi nang sang way bar che ying su dröl,
Release into the expanse all outer, inner, and secret
    impediments.

The expanse is the dharmadhatu. When the dharmadhatu is recognized, one is forever freed from all obstacles. Since we have not yet realized the dharmadhatu, we ask Guru Rinpoche to free us from obstacles through his realization of it. Outer impediments are environmental; inner impediments are physical; secret impediments are mental. This line is the equivalent in this liturgy of the liberation offering, the third feast offering. The next lines are:

> Jang chup bar du drel me je dzin zhing,
> Tse sö nyam tok yar ngo da tar pel,
> Sam pa lhün gyi drup par jin gyi lop,
>
> Care for me beyond separation until awakening;
> Increase life, merit, experiences, and realization like the
>   waxing moon;
> Bless me so that my wishes may be spontaneously fulfilled.

We then end the offering liturgy with Guru Rinpoche's mantra, which is recited once here.

Usually an abbreviated feast liturgy, also written by Mipham Rinpoche, is inserted here. The purpose of repeatedly chanting the abbreviated feast is that by doing so we can accumulate large numbers of feast offerings in order to further accumulate merit. The abbreviated feast liturgy may also be omitted, or simply recited three times.

We begin the abbreviated feast liturgy by consecrating the feast offerings with OM AH HUM HO, recited either three times or once. The first line is:

> Tsa sum lha tsok tsok la chen dren shek,
> Deities of the three roots, come to this feast.

This line is the invitation. The second line is:

> Chi nang sang way de chen tsok chö bül,
> I present outer, inner, and secret feast offerings of great bliss.

Outer, inner, and secret feast offerings are often explained as the offering of a feast to the deities in front, the offering of a feast to the deities within one's body, and the experience of the unity of bliss and emptiness. The deities within our bodies are the peaceful and wrathful deities who are said to appear in the bardo; they are present within our bodies throughout our lives, whether we know it or not. The next line is:

Dam tsik nyam chak tam che töl lo shak,
I admit and confess all violations of samaya.

This line is the feast confession. Feast practice is said to be an excellent occasion for confession. The next line is:

Nyi dzin dra gek chö kyi ying su dröl,
Release dualism, enemies, and obstructors into the
dharmadhatu.

This line is equivalent to the liberation offering, but because of the brevity of this short feast is in the form of a prayer rather than a separate offering. The next line is:

Nyam nyi de wa chen po tuk dam kang,
May our samaya be fulfilled by equality and great bliss.

It could also be read as "May you be satisfied by equality and great bliss." In either case, what pleases Buddhas and fulfills our samaya is realization. Since we have not perfectly realized the equality of the single nature of all things, nor that the realization of this nature is great bliss, this line is an aspiration to do so. The last line is:

Chok dang tün mong ngö drup tsal du söl,
I pray that you grant supreme and common siddhis.

The meaning of this has already been explained.

Then the feast is served and longevity supplications are recited. We recite longevity supplications during the serving of the feast because everything said during a feast has great power.

Then the leftovers are collected and offered. The accompanying lines in this liturgy were extracted by Mipham Rinpoche from the *Embodiment of the Three Jewels*. The leftovers are offered to mundane protectors and other beings unable to receive the first offerings.

The first line of the leftovers offering is:

OM AH HUM. Lhak la wang wa drek pay tsok,
OM AH HUM. Hosts of the haughty, with rights to the leftovers.

Haughty means "powerful" in this line. The second and third lines are:

Trin tar tib shing hap sha gyuk
Sha trak gyen pay tsok lhak zhe

Gather like clouds. Hurry and rush!
Accept these feast leftovers adorned with flesh and blood.

We imagine the leftovers as what will most please those to whom they are offered. Since the beings receiving them are not corporeal human beings, they will experience them as whatever we imagine them to be. The next two lines are:

Ngön gyi dam cha ji zhin du
Ten dra dam nyam ze su zo,

As you promised in the past,
Consume enemies of dharma, samaya corruptors, as your food.

We remind the mundane protectors who receive the leftovers to

fulfill their promise to perform requested activity. The last three
lines are:

> Tak dang tsen ma nyur du tön
> Drup pay bar che dok pa dang
> Trin le tok me drup par dzö.

> Quickly display signs and indications.
> Avert obstacles to accomplishment.
> Accomplish your activity without impediment.

Then we offer the leftovers with the mantra UCCHISHTA BALIMTA
KHAHI: UCCHISHTA means "leftovers," BALIMTA means "torma,"
and KHAHI "eat."

The Empowerment and Conclusion

Then we receive empowerment from Guru Rinpoche. We imagine a white OM in the center of Guru Rinpoche's head at the level of his forehead, a red AH within his throat, and a blue HUM in the center of his body at the level of his heart. These three syllables represent the body, speech, and mind of all Buddhas. From these three syllables emerge rays of the same colors of light. These rays of light dissolve into the corresponding places in our bodies, bestowing upon us the empowerments of body, speech, and mind. This purifies our physical, verbal, and mental obscurations, causing the true nature of our ordinary bodies, speech, and minds to be revealed. The liturgy describing this is:

La may ne sum yi ge dru sum le
Ö zer kar mar ting sum jung ne su
Rang gi ne sum tim pe go sum gyi
Drib jang ku sung tuk kyi dorjer gyur.

From the three syllables in the guru's three places
Emerge rays of white, red, and blue light.

They dissolve into my three places, purifying the stains
Of my three gates, which become the body, speech, and
mind vajras.

The next line is:

Tar ni la ma kor che ö du zhu,
Finally, the guru and his retinue melt into light.

All of the deities surrounding Guru Rinpoche and Yeshe Tsogyal melt into light and dissolve into them. The next line is:

Kar mar tik le hum gi tsen pa ru,
And become a white and red sphere marked by HUM.

After his retinue has dissolved into him, Guru Rinpoche and Yeshe Tsogyal dissolve into one another, melt into light, and become a sphere of light the size of one joint of your thumb. It is white on the outside and red on the inside. In its center is a blue HUM. The last two lines are:

Rang gi nying gar tim pe la may tuk
Rang sem yer me lhen kye chö kur ne A AH.

It dissolves into my heart. The guru's mind and my mind are
indivisible.
I rest in the connate dharmakaya A AH.

The sphere of light, in essence Guru Rinpoche, dissolves into our hearts. We receive his ultimate blessing, and experience the insep-arability of the nature of his mind and the nature of our minds. That nature is the dharmakaya, always present but only recog-nized through devotion.

Mipham Rinpoche concludes with instruction on how to look at the nature of one's mind. He tells us to look at the face of the great primordial dharmakaya, one's mind itself, which has from the very beginning been beyond alteration, transformation, acceptance, and rejection. He then advises us to arise from that with the awareness or view that all appearances, illusory in character, are in nature the display of the guru.

We then conclude the session by dedicating its virtue and proclaiming its auspiciousness.

Shower of Blessings
The Liturgy

༈། །ཚིག་བདུན་གསོལ་འདེབས་དང་འབྲེལ་བའི་བླ་མའི་རྣལ་འབྱོར་བྱིན་རླབས་ཆར་འབེབས་བཞུགས་སོ། །

༁ྀ༔ ཿཧཱུྃཿ ཨོ་རྒྱན་ཡུལ་གྱི་ནུབ་བྱང་མཚམས༔ པདྨ་གེ་སར་སྡོང་པོ་ལ༔ ཡ་མཚན་མཆོག་གི་དངོས་གྲུབ་བརྙེས༔ པདྨ་འབྱུང་གནས་ཞེས་སུ་གྲགས༔ འཁོར་དུ་མཁའ་འགྲོ་མང་པོས་བསྐོར༔ ཁྱེད་ཀྱི་རྗེས་སུ་བདག་བསྒྲུབ་ཀྱི༔ བྱིན་གྱིས་བརླབས་ཕྱིར་གཤེགས་སུ་གསོལ༔ གུ་རུ་པདྨ་སིདྡྷི་ཧཱུྃ༔ རྒྱལ་ཀུན་བསྐྱེད་ཡུམ་ཆོས་དབྱིངས་ཀུན་བཟང་མོ། །ཁོད་འབངས་སྐྱོབ་པའི་མ་ཅིག་དྲིན་མོ་ཆེ། །དངོས་གྲུབ་མཆོག་སྩོལ་བདེ་ཆེན་མཁའ་འགྲོའི་གཙོ། །ཡེ་ཤེས་མཚོ་རྒྱལ་ཞབས་ལ་གསོལ་བ་འདེབས། །ཕྱི་ནང་གསང་བའི་བར་ཆད་ཞི་བ་དང་། །བླ་མའི་སྐུ་ཚེ་བརྟན་པར་བྱིན་གྱིས་རློབས། །ཞད་སྨག་མཚོན་བསྐལ་ཞི་བར་བྱིན་གྱིས་རློབས། །བྱད་ཕུར་ཐོད་གཏོང་ཞི་བར་བྱིན་གྱིས་རློབས། །ཚེ་དཔལ་ཤེས་རབ་རྒྱས་པར་བྱིན་གྱིས་རློབས། །བསམ་པ་ལྷུན་གྱིས་འགྲུབ་པར་བྱིན་གྱིས་རློབས།

།ཅེས་པ་འདི་འང་ཡེ་ཤེས་མཁའ་འགྲོས་བསྐུལ་ངོར་བའི་བུ་མཁའ་ཁྱབ་རྡོ་རྗེས་བྱིས་པ་དགེ་ལེགས་འཕེལ།

ཨཿ རང་ལུས་ཐ་མལ་གནས་པའི་མདུན་མཁའ་རུ། །ཨོ་རྒྱན་དྲི་མེད་དྭངས་ཀྱི་དཔའི་མཚོ། །གཏིང་ཟབ་ཡན་ལག་བརྒྱད་ལྡན་ཆུས་གང་བའི། །དབུས་སུ་རིན་ཆེན་པད་སྡོང་འདབ་རྒྱས་སྟེང་། །སྣ་བས་གནས་ཀུན་འདུས་ཨོ་རྒྱན་རྡོ་རྗེ་འཆང་། །མཚན་དཔེའི་དཔལ་འབར་མཚོ་རྒྱལ་ཡུམ་དང་འཁྲིལ། །ཕྱག་གཡས་རྡོ་རྗེ་གཡོན་པས་ཐོད་བུམ་བསྣམས།

48

Shower of Blessings: A Guruyoga Based on the Seven-Line Prayer

Hum At the northwest border of the land of Uddiyana,
On the center of a lotus stalk,
You achieved amazing supreme siddhi.
You are called Padmakara.
You are surrounded by many dakinis.
I follow your example in accomplishment.
I pray that you come here to grant your blessing.
Guru Padma Siddhi Hum

Mother of all buddhas, dharmadhatu, Samantabhadri,
Only kind mother and protector of Tibetans,
Bestower of supreme siddhi, foremost dakini of mahasukha:
I supplicate at the feet of Yeshe Tsogyal.
Bless us that outer, inner, and secret obstacles be pacified,
That the gurus' lives be stable,
That this age of sickness, famine, and war be pacified,
That curses, kila-magic, and incitements be pacified,
That life, wealth, and wisdom increase,
And that wishes be spontaneously fulfilled.

This was written by Kakyap Dorje, a child nurtured by the wisdom dakini. May goodness increase!

Ah In the sky before my ordinary form
Is the stainless Lake Dhanakosha of Uddiyana.
It is deep and filled with water of eight attributes.
In its midst is a precious lotus in bloom.
Atop it is Uddiyana Vajradhara who embodies all refuges.
With splendid marks and signs he embraces the mother
    Tsogyal.
His right hand holds a vajra, his left a skull and vase.

།དར་དང་རིན་ཆེན་རུས་པའི་རྒྱན་གྱིས་མཛེས། །འོད་ལྡའི་སྐྱོང་ནས་བདེ་ཆེན་
གཟི་བྱིན་འབར། །འཁོར་དུ་རྩ་གསུམ་རྒྱ་མཚོ་སྤྲིན་ལྟར་གཏིབས། །བྱིན་
རླབས་ཕྲགས་རྗེའི་ཆར་འབེབས་བདག་ལ་གཟིགས། །རྒྱལ་ཀུན་དོ་པོ་འཆི་
མེད་ཡེ་ཤེས་སྐུར། །གདུང་ཕྲགས་དྲག་པོས་དད་ཕྱག་རྟག་ཏུ་འཚལ། །ཡིས་
དང་འོངས་སྐྱོད་དུས་གསུམ་དགེ་བའི་ཚོགས། །ཀུན་བཟང་མཆོད་པའི་སྤྲིན་
དུ་དམིགས་ནས་འབུལ། །ཐོག་མེད་ནས་བསགས་སྡིག་ལྟུང་མ་ལུས་
བཤགས། །ཕྱས་བཅས་རྒྱལ་བ་ཀུན་གྱི་ཡོན་ཏན་གྱི། །ཁྱབ་བདག་གཅིག་
པུ་མགོན་པོའི་རྣམ་ཐར་ལ། །སྙིང་ནས་ཡི་རང་དད་པས་གསོལ་འདེབས་ཤིང་
། །ཟབ་རྒྱས་ཆོས་ཀྱི་ཆར་ཆེན་འབེབས་པར་བསྐུལ། །རང་གཞན་དགེ་བའི་
དངོས་པོ་ཀུན་བསྡོམས་ནས། །འགྲོ་ཁམས་རྒྱ་མཚོ་ཇི་སྲིད་གནས་ཀྱི་བར།
།མགོན་པོ་ཁྱོད་ཀྱི་རྣམ་ཐར་རྗེས་སྣེགས་ཏེ། །མཁའ་ཁྱབ་འགྲོ་བ་འདྲེན་པའི་
དོན་དུ་བསྔོ། །སྐྱབས་གནས་ཀུན་འདུས་མ་ཐྲིན་བརྩེའི་གཏེར་ཆེན་པོ།
།དུས་དྲན་སྐྱིགས་མའི་སྐྱབས་མཆོག་རིན་པོ་ཆེ། །ལྷ་བདོའི་རྒྱུད་པས་མནར་
ཞིང་གདུངས་ཕྲགས་ཀྱིས། །གསོལ་འདེབས་བུ་ལ་བརྩེ་བས་ཐུགས་ཀྱིས་
དགོངས། །དགོངས་པའི་སྐྱོང་ནས་ཐུགས་རྗེའི་རྩལ་ཕྱུངས་ལ། །མོས་ལྡན་
བདག་གི་སྙིང་ལ་བྱིན་གྱིས་རློབས། །ཧྲགས་དང་མཆན་མ་སྨྱུར་དུ་སྤྲིན་པ་དང་
། །མཆོག་དང་ཐུན་མོང་དངོས་གྲུབ་སྩལ་དུ་གསོལ། ཞེས་བྱས་ལ་ཚོག་
བདུན་གསོལ་འདེབས་ཅི་ནུས་སུ་འདོན། ཧཱུྃ༔ ཨོ་རྒྱན་ཡུལ་གྱི་ནུབ་བྱང་མཚམས༔
པདྨ་གེ་སར་སྡོང་པོ་ལ༔ ཡ་མཚན་མཆོག་གི་དངོས་གྲུབ་བརྙེས༔

He is adorned by silk, jewels, and bone.
In an expanse of the five lights, he is magnificent with great bliss.
The oceans of the three roots surround him like clouds.
Raining down blessing and compassion, he gazes at me.

To the immortal wisdom body of all victors
I always prostrate with intense faith and yearning.
I offer my body, possessions, and virtues of the three times,
Imagining them as Samantabhadra's offering clouds.
I confess all wrongdoing and downfalls from
    beginningless time.
I rejoice from my heart in your deeds, only all-pervasive lord
Of the virtues of all victors and their children. I pray to you
    with faith.
I request that you shower us with dharma profound and deep.
I dedicate all the virtue of myself and others to this:
For as long as the oceans of beings remain,
May I emulate your deeds, my lord,
And be a guide to all beings throughout space.

Embodiment of all refuges, great treasury of wisdom and love,
Invaluable protector of beings during bad and decadent times:
Think with love of this child who prays to you
With my mind tormented by fivefold degeneration.
From the expanse of your wisdom, let loose the power of
    compassion.
I am devoted to you. Bless my heart.
Quickly display signs and indications.
I pray that you grant supreme and common siddhi.

HUM At the northwest border of the land of Uddiyana,
On the center of a lotus stalk,
You achieved amazing supreme siddhi.

པད་འབྱུང་གནས་ཞེས་སུ་གྲགས༔ འབོར་དུ་མཁའ་འགྲོ་མང་པོས་བསྐོར༔

ཁྱེད་ཀྱི་རྗེས་སུ་བདག་བསྒྲུབ་ཀྱིས༔ བྱིན་གྱིས་རློབས་ཕྱིར་གཤེགས་སུ་

གསོལ༔ གུ་རུ་པདྨ་སི་ཏྟི་ཧཱུྂ༔

མོས་གུས་ཀྱིས་གསོལ་བ་བཏབ་པས་བླ་མ་ཡབ་ཡུམ་གྱི་སྤྱིར་མཚམས་དང་ཕྱགས་ཀ་

ནས་ཡེ་ཤེས་ཀྱི་འོད་ཟེར་སྣ་ལྔ་བ་ཐག་ལྤར་བཀྱུངས་ནས་རང་གི་སྙིང་གར་ཐིམ་པས་

རྒྱུན་བྱིན་གྱིས་བརླབ་པར་བསམ། བརྫ་གུ་རུ་ཙེ་རིགས་བཟླ། ཚོགས་མཆོད་སྟོན་

ཟུར་གསལ་སྟར། རྒྱུན་དུ་དབང་ལེན་ལ་འདུག ཌྷོ་རྗེའི་ཚོགས་བདུན་དང་འབྲེལ་བའི་

ཚོགས་མཆོད་དཔལ་གྱི་ཐུམ་བཟང་བཞུགས་སོ། །ཁ་ཅང་སོགས་ཙེ་འགྱོར་བའི་དམ་

རྫས་བཤམས་ལ།

ཧཱུྂ༔ ཨ་ལས་ཚོས་དབྱིངས་དང་མཉམ་ཀ་པཱ་ལར། །ཨོྃ་ལས་སྣང་སྲིད་འདོད་

ཡོན་ཚོགས་སུ་བཤམས། །ཧཱུྂ་གིས་བདེ་ཆེན་ཡེ་ཤེས་རོལ་པར་བསྒྱུར། །ཧྲཱིཿཡིས་རུ་

གསུམ་ལྷ་ཚོགས་དགྱེས་པ་བསྐང༌། །ཨོྃ་ཨཱཿཧཱུྂ་ཧྲཱི། བྱིན་གྱིས་

བརླབས། ཚོགས་ཞིང་སྐུན་འདྲེན་ཅིང་མཆོད་པ་འབུལ་བ་ནི།

You are called Padmakara.
You are surrounded by many dakinis.
I follow your example in accomplishment.
I pray that you come here to grant your blessing.
GURU PADMA SIDDHI HUM

Recite the Seven-Line Prayer as much as you can. Think that through your devoted prayer, fivefold rays of wisdom light like strings emerge from the union of the father and mother gurus and from their hearts. These dissolve into your heart, blessing you. Recite the Vajra Guru as much as appropriate. If you wish, insert the feast offering I have written separately. In daily practice, proceed with the empowerment.

THE GLORIOUS VASE: A FEAST OFFERING BASED ON THE SEVEN-LINE PRAYER

Set out whatever samaya substances are available, such as meat and liquor.

HUM From A arises a kapala equal to the dharmadhatu.
From OM arises all that appears and exists, set out as a
   desirable feast.
With HUM it is transformed into the play of the wisdom of
   great bliss.
With HRIH it fills the deities of the three roots with pleasure.
OM AH HUM HRIH

Bless it with that.

Then the invitation to the feast assembly, and the presentation of offerings:

ཧཱུྃཿ ཨོ་རྒྱན་ཡུལ་གྱི་ནུབ་བྱང་མཚམསཿ པདྨ་གེ་སར་སྡོང་པོ་ལཿ ཡ་མཚན་
མཆོག་གི་དངོས་གྲུབ་བརྙེསཿ པདྨ་འབྱུང་གནས་ཞེས་སུ་གྲགསཿ འཁོར་དུ་
མཁའ་འགྲོ་མང་པོས་བསྐོརཿ ཁྱེད་ཀྱི་རྗེས་སུ་བདག་བསྒྲུབ་ཀྱིསཿ འདོད་
ཡོན་ཚོགས་ལ་སྤྱན་འདྲེན་ནཿ བྱིན་གྱིས་རློབས་ཕྱིར་གཤེགས་སུ་གསོལཿ
གནས་མཆོག་འདི་རུ་བྱིན་ཕོབ་ལཿ ཚོགས་མཆོད་ཡེ་ཤེས་བདུད་རྩིར་བསྒྱུརཿ
སྒྲུབ་མཆོག་བདག་ལ་དབང་བཞི་བསྐུརཿ བགེགས་དང་ལོག་འདྲེན་བར་ཆད་
སོལཿ མཆོག་དང་ཐུན་མོང་དངོས་གྲུབ་སྩོལཿ ཧཱུྃ། བླ་མ་རྗེ་བཙུན་པདྨ་ཧོ༔
ཕྱིང་རྩལ། །རིག་འཛིན་མཁའ་འགྲོའི་ཚོགས་དང་བཅས་པ་ཡི། །རྩ་གསུམ་
ཀུན་འདུས་རྒྱལ་བའི་དཀྱིལ་འཁོར་ལ། །མོས་གུས་གདུང་ཤུགས་དྲག་པོས་
གསོལ་བ་འདེབས། །བདག་གཞན་སྒོ་གསུམ་དགེ་ཚོགས་ལོངས་སྤྱོད་བཅས།
།སྣང་སྲིད་འདོད་ཡོན་དགྱེས་དགུ་མ་ཚང་མེད། །ཀུན་བཟང་བདེ་ཆེན་ཚོགས་
ཀྱི་འཁོར་ལོར་འབུལ། །ཕྱགས་བརྗེའི་དགྱེས་བཞེས་ཕྱགས་དམ་བསྐོང་གྱུར་
ཅིག །གསོལ་བ་འདེབས་སོ་གུ་རུ་རིན་པོ་ཆེ། །བྱིན་གྱིས་རློབས་ཤིག་རིག
འཛིན་མཁའ་འགྲོའི་ཚོགས། །མོས་ལྡན་བུ་ལ་མཆོག་ཐུན་དངོས་གྲུབ་སྩོལ།
།དམ་ཚིག་ཉམས་ཆགས་ཐམས་ཅད་སྐྱོངས་དུ་གསོལ། །ཕྱི་ནང་གསང་བའི་
བར་ཆད་དབྱིངས་སུ་སྐྲོལ། །བྱང་ཆུབ་བར་དུ་འབྲལ་མེད་རྗེས་འཛིན་ཞིང་།
།ཚེ་བསོད་ཉམས་རྟོགས་ཡར་ངོའི་ཟླ་ལྟར་འཕེལ།

HUM At the northwest border of the land of Uddiyana,
On the center of a lotus stalk,
You achieved amazing supreme siddhi.
You are called Padmakara.
You are surrounded by many dakinis.
I follow your example in accomplishment.
If I invite you to this desirable feast,
I pray that you come here to grant your blessing.
Bless this best of places.
Transform this feast into wisdom amrita.
Grant me, a practitioner, the four empowerments.
Remove obstructors, corruptors, and impediments.
Grant supreme and common siddhi.

HUM Guru, Lord Padma Tötrengtsal,
With your assembly of vidyadharas and dakinis,
You are a mandala of victors that embodies all the three roots.
I pray to you with intense devotion and yearning.
I offer you my own and others' three gates, virtues, and
    possessions;
All appearance and existence; and everything desirable and
    pleasing,
As a ganachakra of Samantabhadra's great bliss.
Kindly accept it. May you be satisfied.
Guru Rinpoche, I pray to you.
Bless me, vidyadharas and dakinis.
Grant your devoted child supreme and common siddhi.
I pray that you purify all violations of samaya.
Release into the expanse all outer, inner, and secret
    impediments.
Care for me beyond separation until awakening.
Increase life, merit, experiences, and realization like the
    waxing moon.

།བསམ་པ་ལྷུན་གྱིས་འགྲུབ་པར་བྱིན་གྱིས་རློབས། །ཨོཾ་ཨཱཿཧཱུྃ་བཛྲ་གུ་རུ་པདྨ་སིདྡྷི་ཧཱུྃ།

། །ཚོགས་བསྐང་ནི། ཚོགས་རྫས་རྣམས། ཨོཾ་ཨཱཿཧཱུྃ་དོས། བྱིན་གྱིས་རླབས། རུ་གསུམ་ལྷ་ཚོགས་ཚོགས་ལ་སྤྱན་འདྲེན་གཤེགས། །ཕྱི་ནང་གསང་བའི་བདེ་ཆེན་ཚོགས་མཆོད་འབུལ། ངོར་སེམས་ལྷ་བུ་ཁ་བསྐྱར། །དམ་ཚིག་ཉམས་ཆགས་ཐམས་ཅད་མཐོལ་ལོ་བཤགས། །གཉིས་འཛིན་དགྲ་བགེགས་ཚོགས་ཀྱི་དབྱིངས་སུ་སྒྲོལ། །མཉམ་ཉིད་བདེ་བ་ཆེན་པོའི་ཕྱགས་དམ་བསྐངས། །མཆོག་དང་ཐུན་མོང་དངོས་གྲུབ་བསྩལ་དུ་གསོལ། །ཞེས་པའང་ཚོགས་གྲངས་བསགས་སོགས་ལ་འཁོ་བའི་ཚོགས་བསྐངས་འཛམ་དཔལ་རྡོ་རྗེས་སོ།། །།

ཨོཾ་ཨཱཿཧཱུྃ༔ ལྷག་ལ་དབང་བ་རྗེགས་པའི་ཚོགས༔ སྟིན་ལྷར་བཅིབས་ཤིང་ ཆབ་ག་རྒྱག༔ ག་ཁྲག་རྒྱན་པའི་ཚོགས་ལྷག་བཞེས༔ སྟོན་གྱི་དམ་བཅའ་རྗེ་ བཞིན་དུ༔ བསྟན་དགྲ་དམ་ཉམས་ཟས་སུ་ཟོ༔ རྣགས་དང་མཆན་མ་སྨྱུར་དུ་ སྟོན༔ བསྒྲུབ་པའི་བར་ཆད་བསྲོག་པ་དང༔ ཕྱིན་ལས་ཐོགས་མེད་འགྲུབ་ པར་མཛོད༔ ཨུ་ཙྪི་བ་ལིང་ཏ་ཁཱ་ཧི༔ ཞེས་བརྗོད་ནས་ལྷག་མ་དོར་རོ། །ཕྱན་ མཐར།

Bless me so that my wishes may be spontaneously fulfilled.
OM AH HUM VAJRA GURU PADMA SIDDHI HUM

AN ABBREVIATED FEAST

Bless the feast with OM AH HUM HO

Deities of the three roots, come to this feast.
(Substitute "Vajrasattva" etc. for "the three roots.")
I present outer, inner, and secret feast offerings of great bliss.
I admit and confess all violations of samaya.
Release dualism, enemies, and obstructors into the
    dharmadhatu.
Be fulfilled by equality, great bliss.
I pray that you grant supreme and common siddhis.

*This abbreviated feast was written by Jampal Dorje for use in
the accumulation of feasts and so forth.*

OM AH HUM Hosts of the haughty, with right to the leftovers,
Gather like clouds. Hurry and rush!
Accept these feast leftovers adorned by flesh and blood.
As you promised in the past,
Consume enemies of dharma, samaya corruptors, as your food.
Quickly display signs and indications.
Avert obstacles to accomplishment.
Accomplish your activity without impediment.
UCCHISHTA BALIMTA KHAHI

Saying that, carry out the leftovers.

At the session's end:

བླ་མའི་གནས་གསུམ་ཡི་གེ་འབྲུ་གསུམ་ལས། །འོད་ཟེར་དཀར་དམར་མཐིང་
གསུམ་བྱུང་ནས་སུ། །རང་གི་གནས་གསུམ་ཐིམ་པས་སྒྲོ་གསུམ་གྱི། །སྒྲིབ་
བྱང་སྐུ་གསུང་ཐུགས་ཀྱི་རྡོ་རྗེར་གྱུར། །མཐར་ནི་བླ་མ་འཁོར་བཅས་འོད་དུ་
ཞུ། །དཀར་དམར་ཐིག་ལེ་ཧཱུྃ་གིས་མཚོན་པ་རུ། །རང་གི་སྙིང་གར་ཐིམ་པས་
བླ་མའི་ཐུགས། །རང་སེམས་དབྱེར་མེད་ལྷན་སྐྱེས་ཆོས་སྐུར་གནས། ༀ་ཨྃཿ

།ཞེས་བརྗོད་ལ་ཡེ་ནས་བཅོས་བསྒྱུར་སྤང་བླང་ལས་འདས་པ་རང་གི་སེམས་ཉིད་
གདོད་མའི་ཆོས་སྐུ་ཆེན་པོའི་རང་ཞལ་བལྟ། །སྐུར་ཡང་སྐྱ་མ་ལྟ་བུའི་སྡུང་བ་ཐམས་
ཅད་བླ་མའི་རང་བཞིན་དུ་བསྒྱུར་ལ་དགེ་བ་བསྔོ་ཞིང་ཤིས་པ་བརྗོད་པས་བདེ་ལེགས་
སུ་བྱའོ། །ཞེས་པའང་ཐམས་ཅད་འདུལ་ཞེས་པའི་གྲོ་བཞིན་བླ་བའི་ཡར་ཆོས་བཀྱད་
ལ། ཚེ་རབས་ཐམས་ཅད་དུ་གུ་རུ་པདྨའི་ཐན་དུ་སྐྱོན་ལས་འདའབས་པ་མི་ཐམ་རྣམ་
པར་རྒྱལ་བའི་ཡིད་ཀྱི་མཚོ་ལས་བྱུང་བ་དགེའོ། །སརྦ་མངྒ་ལོ།

From the three syllables in the guru's three places
Emerge rays of white, red, and blue light.
They dissolve into my three places, purifying the stains
Of my three gates, which become the body, speech, and
   mind vajras.
Finally, the guru and retinue melt into light
And become a white and red sphere marked by Hum.
It dissolves into my heart. The guru's mind and my mind
   are indivisible.
I rest in the connate dharmakaya A Ah.

Saying that, look at the face of your own nature. Unaltered and unchanged from the beginning, it is beyond acceptance and rejection. Your mind itself is the primordial great dharmakaya.

Afterward view all illusory appearances as the nature of the guru. Dedicate the virtue and cause goodness by expressing auspiciousness.

On the eighth day of the waxing phase of the month Shravana, called All-Subduing, this arose from the lake of the mind of Mipham Nampar Gyalwa, who prays to serve Guru Padma in every life. Sarva Mangalam

About KTD Publications
Gathering the Garlands of the Gurus' Precious Teachings

KTD Publications is the Karmapa's press in the West and is a part of Karma Triyana Dharmachakra (KTD) in Woodstock, NY. We are a not-for-profit publisher established with the purpose of facilitating and fulfilling the projects and activities of the 17th Gyalwang Karmapa Ogyen Trinley Dorje. Our focus is on works that have never before been published, works that have never before been translated into English, and special edition books.

Visit us at www.ktdpublications.com

Books by Lama Yeshe Gyamtso

Lama Yeshe's published translations include *Chariot of the Fortunate: The Life of Yongey Mingyur Rinpoche*; *The Vajra Garland and the Lotus Garden: Treasure Biographies of Padmakara and Vairochana*; *Nyima Tashi: The Songs and Instructions of the First Traleg Kyabgon Rinpoche*; *Treasury of Eloquence: The Songs of Barway Dorje*; *The Precious Essence*; *Amrita of Eloquence: A Biography of Khenpo Karthar Rinpoche*; *Garland of Jewels: The Eight Bodhisattvas*; *The Hundred Tertöns*, *Siddhas of Ga: Remembered by Khenpo Karthar Rinpoche*; and author of *On the Four Noble Truths*.